Little People, BIG DREAMS™
MARILYN MONROE

Written by
Maria Isabel Sánchez Vegara

Illustrated by
Ana Albero

Frances Lincoln
Children's Books

Once, in the city of Los Angeles, there was a little girl with lots of love to give. Her name was Norma Jeane. Her mother was sick in hospital for most of her childhood, so she was raised in orphanages and with foster families.

Some of the families she lived with would send her to the movies. Norma Jeane loved losing herself in the big black and white screen. For her, it was more colorful than the world around her.

She was just sixteen when she got married to her neighbor, James. But Norma Jeane soon realised that being a housewife was not her thing. When James was sent away with the Marines, she couldn't help but feel relieved.

Norma Jeane got a job spraying plane parts in a factory. There she met a photographer who took pictures of female workers for the army. Her first shoot came naturally to her... and before long, she became a model!

In less than two years, Norma Jeane appeared on more than 30 covers! She was one of the most popular models at her agency, and she loved her job. But still, she felt she was born to do more…

At home, looking out on the Hollywood night, Norma Jeane thought about the thousands of girls just like her who were dreaming about becoming a movie star. She decided not to worry—she knew she was dreaming the hardest.

Eager to become a star, she dyed her hair light blonde and chose a name that sounded just fabulous: Marilyn Monroe. With her explosive look and bright personality, she was ready to try to make it as an actress.

For half a year, she didn't get any roles, but that didn't bother her. Marilyn dedicated the time to acting, singing, and dancing lessons. She also spent lots of time at the studio, trying to learn from others as much as she could.

Marilyn was finally picked for a blockbuster called *All About Eve*. She felt tiny next to the great Bette Davis—one of the world's most respected actresses—but she held her head high. Soon, people wanted to know everything about her!

When America found out she had posed with very little clothes on for a calendar, the studio she worked for asked her to deny it. But Marilyn knew she had done nothing wrong and told the truth, gaining everyone's respect and understanding.

Marilyn became a fabulous personality, who thought it was better to be absolutely ridiculous than absolutely boring.

She was one of the first women to own a production company,
fighting for equal roles and salaries for actresses and actors.

But, even though she was the most famous star in Hollywood, she still remembered how it felt to be lonely. When she was invited to go overseas to entertain the troops and visit the soldiers at the hospital, she didn't think twice.

And after giving her best in more than 20 movies, little
Norma Jeane, the girl who never belonged to anything
or anyone, found her home in the hearts of the people—
the place where she will belong forever.

MARILYN MONROE

(Born 1926 – Died 1962)

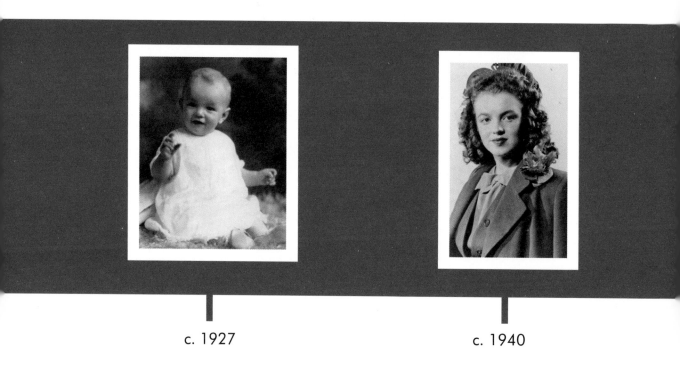

c. 1927   c. 1940

The star we know today as Marilyn Monroe was born as Norma Jeane Mortenson. When she was seven, her mother went into hospital, meaning that Norma Jeane spent much of her childhood in orphanages and many different foster homes. She fell in love with movies at local picture houses and dreamed of becoming the stars she saw on screens and magazine covers. Aged 16, her foster parents decided to move away from California and Norma Jeane chose to marry her neighbor, James Dougherty, rather than return to foster care. When he left to work for the Marines, Norma took a job on the assembly line at an airplane factory in Burbank, California. Photographer David Conover saw her while taking pictures of women contributing to the war effort. In an instant, he knew that she was

1948   1957

a natural: a "photographer's dream." Marilyn began studying the work of
legendary actresses Jean Harlow and Lana Turner, and enrolled in drama
classes. From 1950, she worked steadily in films. When it was discovered
that Marilyn had posed for a calendar with not many clothes on, it was a
scandal—but she told the truth about her involvement, and her fame grew
even bigger. Using her fame and love for people, Marilyn traveled the
world, performing for audiences of all kinds: war-weary troops, Hollywood
crowds... and even John F Kennedy on his 45th birthday! She started her
own motion picture company before the age of thirty. At the 1962 Golden
Globes, Marilyn was named female World Film Favorite, once again
showing just how much she was loved by people all over the world.

Want to find out more about Marilyn Monroe?

Have a read of this great book:

Making Their Voices Heard: The Inspiring Friendship of Ella Fitzgerald and Marilyn Monroe by Vivian Kirkfield

Brimming with creative inspiration, how-to projects, and useful information to enrich your everyday life, Quarto Knows is a favourite destination for those pursuing their interests and passions. Visit our site and dig deeper with our books into your area of interest: Quarto Creates, Quarto Cooks, Quarto Homes, Quarto Lives, Quarto Drives, Quarto Explores, Quarto Gifts, or Quarto Kids.

Published by Katie Cotton • Designed by Karissa Santos
Edited by Katy Flint and Rachel Williams • Production by Nikki Ingram
Editorial Assistance from Alex Hithersay and Rachel Robinson
Manufactured in Guangdong, China CC062021
1 3 5 7 9 8 6 4 2

Photographic acknowledgements (pages 28-29, from left to right): 1. Studio portrait of American actor Marilyn Monroe (born Norma Jean Mortenson, 1926 - 1962) at the age of six months, sitting on a woolly rug in a white smock © Hulton Archive via Getty Image. 2. A teenaged Norma Jeane Baker, future film star Marilyn Monroe (1926 - 1962), circa 1940 © Silver Screen Collection/Hulton Archive via Getty Images. 3. Marilyn Monroe as she appears in the 1948 musical Ladies of the Chorus, playing the lead role of dancer Peggy Martin © George Rinhart/Corbis via Getty Image. 4. Marilyn Monroe laughs as she poses wearing an amber bead necklace in 1957 in Amagansett, New York © Sam Shaw/Shaw Family Archives via Getty Images

Collect the *Little People*, **BIG DREAMS**™ series:

FRIDA KAHLO	COCO CHANEL	MAYA ANGELOU	AMELIA EARHART	AGATHA CHRISTIE	MARIE CURIE	ROSA PARKS

AUDREY HEPBURN	EMMELINE PANKHURST	ELLA FITZGERALD	ADA LOVELACE	JANE AUSTEN	GEORGIA O'KEEFFE	HARRIET TUBMAN

ANNE FRANK	MOTHER TERESA	JOSEPHINE BAKER	L. M. MONTGOMERY	JANE GOODALL	SIMONE DE BEAUVOIR	MUHAMMAD ALI

STEPHEN HAWKING	MARIA MONTESSORI	VIVIENNE WESTWOOD	MAHATMA GANDHI	DAVID BOWIE	WILMA RUDOLPH	DOLLY PARTON

BRUCE LEE	RUDOLF NUREYEV	ZAHA HADID	MARY SHELLEY	MARTIN LUTHER KING JR.	DAVID ATTENBOROUGH	ASTRID LINDGREN

EVONNE GOOLAGONG	BOB DYLAN	ALAN TURING	BILLIE JEAN KING	GRETA THUNBERG	JESSE OWENS	JEAN-MICHEL BASQUIAT

ARETHA FRANKLIN

CORAZON AQUINO

PELÉ

ERNEST SHACKLETON

STEVE JOBS

AYRTON SENNA

LOUISE BOURGEOIS

ELTON JOHN

JOHN LENNON

PRINCE

CHARLES DARWIN

CAPTAIN TOM MOORE

HANS CHRISTIAN ANDERSEN

STEVIE WONDER

MEGAN RAPINOE

MARY ANNING

MALALA YOUSAFZAI

ANDY WARHOL

RUPAUL

MICHELLE OBAMA

MINDY KALING

IRIS APFEL

ROSALIND FRANKLIN

RUTH BADER GINSBURG

MARILYN MONROE

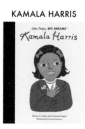

KAMALA HARRIS

ALBERT EINSTEIN

ACTIVITY BOOKS

STICKER ACTIVITY BOOK

COLORING BOOK

LITTLE ME, BIG DREAMS JOURNAL

Discover more about the series at www.littlepeoplebigdreams.com